MAX AXIOM
AND THE SOCIETY OF SUPER SCIENTISTS

ANIMAL EXTINCTION
EMERGENCY

WRITTEN BY **EMILY SOHN**
ILLUSTRATED BY **EDUARDO GARCIA**
COVER ART BY **ERIK DOESCHER**

Raintree is an imprint of Capstone Global Library Limited, a
company incorporated in England and Wales having its registered
office at 264 Banbury Road, Oxford, OX2 7DY – Registered company
number: 6695582

www.raintree.co.uk
myorders@raintree.co.uk

Edited by Abby Huff and Aaron Sautter
Designed by Brann Harvey
Original illustrations © Capstone Global Library Limited 2022
Production by Laura Manthe
Originated by Capstone Global Library Ltd
Printed and bound in India

978 1 3982 3384 3

British Library Cataloguing in Publication Data
A full catalogue record for this book is available from the British
Library.

CONTENTS

THE SOCIETY OF
SUPER SCIENTISTS

MAX AXIOM

After years of study, Max Axiom, the world's first Super Scientist, knew the mysteries of the universe were too vast for one person alone to uncover. So Max created the Society of Super Scientists! Using their superpowers and super-brains, this talented group investigates today's most urgent scientific and environmental issues and learns about actions everyone can take to solve them.

LIZZY AXIOM

NICK AXIOM

SPARK

THE DISCOVERY LAB

Home of the Society of Super Scientists, this state-of-the-art lab houses advanced tools for cutting-edge research and radical scientific innovation. More importantly, it is a space for Super Scientists to collaborate and share knowledge as they work together to tackle any challenge.

Super Scientists Max Axiom and his nephew Nick are walking through the rainforest to look for unique creatures. But they soon discover an animal emergency instead . . .

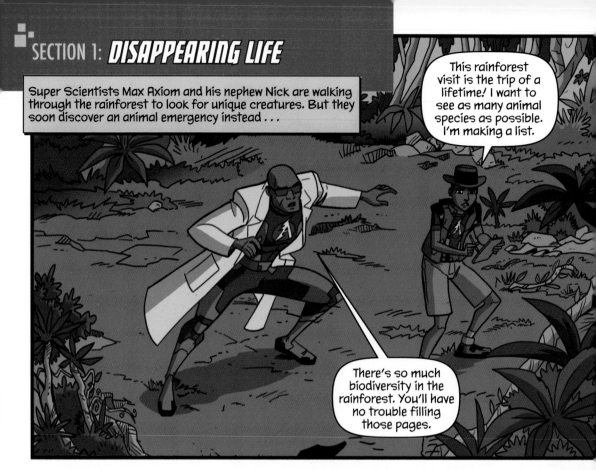

This rainforest visit is the trip of a lifetime! I want to see as many animal species as possible. I'm making a list.

There's so much biodiversity in the rainforest. You'll have no trouble filling those pages.

BZZZ! BZZZZ!

Lizzy, why are you calling from Discovery Lab?

Max! Nick! There's been an incident near you. Poison dart frogs are being poached!

Poached? You mean someone has stolen poison dart frogs from the forest?

Yes, and that's not all. These frogs are an endangered species.

They're at risk of dying out completely.

Don't worry, Lizzy. We'll check out this creature crisis!

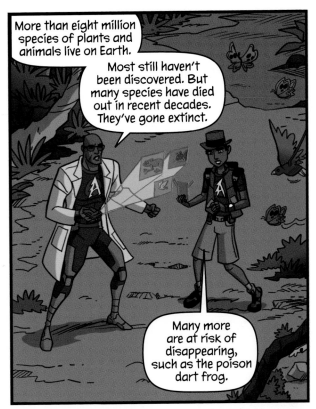

More than eight million species of plants and animals live on Earth.

Most still haven't been discovered. But many species have died out in recent decades. They've gone extinct.

Many more are at risk of disappearing, such as the poison dart frog.

So, why would the poison dart frog and other species be at risk, and what can we do to help?

To answer those questions, we need to know more about why extinctions happen in the first place. Let's start by travelling back in time to about 100 million years ago, when dinosaurs roamed the Earth.

TRACKING SPECIES' STATUS

The International Union for Conservation of Nature (IUCN) keeps track of how species are faring. The IUCN Red List is the official source of their status. There are nine categories. On one end are extinct and extinct in the wild (but still living in protected places). Then comes critically endangered, endangered, vulnerable, near threatened and least concern. The last two categories, data deficient and not evaluated, are used to list species for which too little information is known.

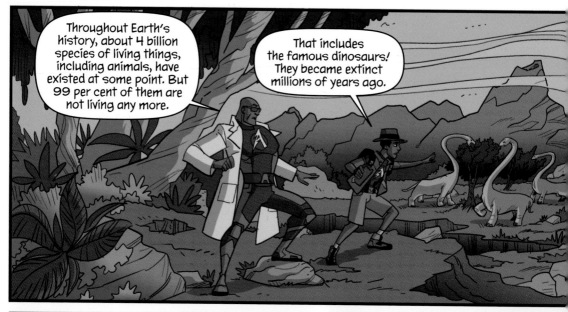

Throughout Earth's history, about 4 billion species of living things, including animals, have existed at some point. But 99 per cent of them are not living any more.

That includes the famous dinosaurs! They became extinct millions of years ago.

Species can become extinct for many reasons. Sometimes, extinctions are a normal part of life. Causes can include sudden changes on Earth and diseases.

The dinosaurs' time ended 66 million years ago. A major clue about what happened to them came in the 1990s.

Researchers found signs of the huge Chicxulub crater off Yucatán Peninsula in Mexico.

The crater is evidence that a giant asteroid about 9.6 kilometres, or 6 miles, wide struck our planet. It's estimated it was going at 64,000 km, or 40,000 miles, per hour. The impact was catastrophic.

The end of the dinosaurs is called the Cretaceous-Tertiary, or K-T, extinction event. Lots of other species went extinct at the same time.

Shock waves from the strike led to earthquakes and volcanic eruptions. Tsunamis washed over continents. Debris darkened the skies for months or years.

Temperatures dropped, killing plants. Without plants to eat, herbivores soon died out. Then carnivores went extinct too.

The good news is that an asteroid of that size doesn't hit Earth very often.

But the bad news?

Scientists call the end of the dinosaurs a "mass extinction event" because so many species died out at once. It wasn't the first mass extinction event. And it won't be the last.

Extinctions often come in waves. By looking at fossils, scientists know there have been five mass extinction events so far.

445-415 MILLION YEARS AGO: The first known mass extinction event. Earth's climate changed and cooled, causing 85 per cent of all species to die out.

380-359 MILLION YEARS AGO: Volcanic activity and climate change caused changes in the ocean that led to the loss of 75 per cent of species.

251 MILLION YEARS AGO: The biggest known extinction. Volcanoes, wildfires and other changes doomed about 96 per cent of species.

201 MILLION YEARS AGO: With great warming of Earth, 80 per cent of species disappeared.

66 MILLION YEARS AGO: The event that ended the dinosaurs and other species.

TIMELINE OF EARTH LIFE

- Simple life began 3.7 billion years ago
- First animals appeared 800 million years ago
- Dinosaurs appeared 245 million years ago
- Dinosaurs went extinct 66 million years ago
- Early humans appeared 5 to 7 million years ago
- Modern humans appeared about 400,000 years ago

Big changes started happening on Earth about 10,000 years ago. That sounds like a long time ago. But . . .

In "Earth time", that's nothing!

We're at the end of the last Ice Age. Ice ages are cold periods when much of Earth is covered by huge ice sheets. As the ice melted, humans started spreading out across the land.

When people moved to new places, their behaviour affected more animals. This is still true today. As the number of people on Earth grows, so does our impact.

Hunting is one obvious way people affect animals. But there are other ways in which human activity harms animals too.

Welcome to Mauritius in the 1640s! It's a small island near Madagascar. Max, may I introduce you to the dodo?

That's a big bird!

It *was* big. Dodos are extinct in our time. But when they lived, a typical dodo was 0.9 metres, or 3 feet, tall.

Dodos lived only on the island of Mauritius. They couldn't fly and they hadn't learned to be afraid of people. When European sailors arrived in the 1500s, the birds were easy to hunt. People also destroyed the dodo's habitat to build homes.

People brought other animals to the island, too, like pigs. Those animals ate dodo eggs. They also ate food that the dodos ate. That left dodos without enough to eat.

The last known sighting of a dodo was in 1662. Within 100 years of people arriving on the island, the dodos were all gone.

PASSENGER PIGEONS
Extinct due to:
hunting

THYLACINE
(aka Tasmanian tiger)
Extinct due to: hunting,
habitat destruction, disease

WEST AFRICAN BLACK RHINO
Extinct due to:
poaching

There are many more stories like the dodo. Passenger pigeons, thylacines and West African black rhinos are just a few species that have recently become extinct.

Many more species are close to the edge, such as pandas, Asian elephants and vaquita porpoises.

PANDAS
At risk due to:
poaching, deforestation

ASIAN ELEPHANTS
At risk due to:
habitat loss, poaching

VAQUITA PORPOISE
At risk due to:
illegal fishing

It seems like more and more animals are disappearing or at risk. And people are a big reason why.

We've learned a lot from our field investigation. Let's go and see what Lizzy has found out at the lab.

Max! Nick! How's your research going?

Hi, Lizzy! We've learned about mass extinctions and gathered clues about what causes species to disappear.

What have you discovered?

I've found out that where an animal lives can put them at greater risk.

Islands are tough because animals can't always leave if there's a threat. The arrival of people and invasive species can quickly wipe them out.

Maybe dodos would still be around if they had been able to get away from people.

Species that can only survive under certain conditions face trouble when those conditions change.

Some animals eat only one kind of food. For example, koalas eat only eucalyptus leaves.

If people cut down the forests where their food grows, the animals will starve.

With all the threats facing the poison dart frog and other animals, it could take a lot of effort to save them.

True, but there are also many reasons to keep fighting extinction.

One reason is that nature is all about balance. Losing one species often affects others connected to it.

Take food chains and food webs, for example. If you lose a predator, the populations of its prey may grow for a time. But then those animals might eat all of their own food source and die off too.

PREDATOR

PREY

PLANTS

GETTING INVOLVED

Conservation isn't just for adults. There are plenty of ways children can learn how to help protect many living animals and their habitats. Check out the list below for different activities and opportunities. Try a few, or get inspired to start something new. Thanks for helping out!

▶ National Geographic list their top five ways you can help to save the planet, including how to save water, think about where your food comes from and recycle your waste.
www.natgeokids.com/uk/discover/science/nature/how-to-save-the-planet/

▶ Earth Hour is held every year. Millions of homes across the world switch off their non-essential lights for one hour in order to conserve energy. You can join in!
www.wwf.org.uk/earth-hour

▶ Want to protect the oceans? Become armed with ocean wildlife facts and take note of your plastic use.
www.wwf.org.uk/sites/default/files/2019-08/WWF_Oceans_and_Plastics_KS2_Activities.pdf

▶ Learn how to grow your own fruit and vegetables.
www.bbcgoodfood.com/howto/guide/easy-crops-kids-grow

▶ Find out what you will need to do your own litter picking at the beach.
www.wildlifewatch.org.uk/go-litter-pick-or-beach-clean

▶ Make a bee hotel for your garden.
www.wildlifetrusts.org/actions/how-make-bee-hotel

▶ A lot of volunteer opportunities will be unique to where you live. To find ways to join in, try contacting local organizations or local branches of national organizations, such as:

- Nature Volunteers:
www.naturevolunteers.uk

- RSPB:
www.rspb.org.uk/get-involved/volunteering-fundraising/volunteer/

- The Conservation Volunteers:
www.tcv.org.uk

- The Wildlife Trusts:
www.wildlifetrusts.org/closer-to-nature/volunteer

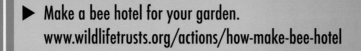

GLOSSARY

biodiversity number and variety of plants and animals that are found in an area

catastrophic describing a violent and extremely destructive event

conservation protection of Earth's natural resources, such as water, forests and wildlife

endangered at risk of dying out and with few individuals left

extinct no longer living

habitat natural place and conditions in which a plant or animal lives

invasive not native to an area and may cause harm to the environment into which it was brought

migration regular movement of animals as they search different places for food

poach take a plant or animal from a place where it is illegal to do so

regulations rules or laws

reproduce make offspring; many animals reproduce by mating

species group of living things that share common characteristics

FIND OUT MORE

Endangered Rainforests: Investigating Rainforests in Crisis (Endangered Earth), Rani Iyer (Raintree, 2020)

Saving British Wildlife: Success Stories, Claire Throp (Raintree, 2019)

Saving Endangered Animals (Beyond the Headlines!), Jilly Hunt (Raintree, 2017)

WEBSITES

www.countryfile.com/wildlife/10-of-the-most-endangered-animal-species-in-britain/
Find out which British animal species are the most endangered.

www.wildlifewatch.org.uk/facts-and-stories/environment
Wildlife Watch shows you how to make a difference to your local environment.

INDEX